TWIST IN MY TALES
Short Stories for Children

Marie Watts

MINERVA PRESS
LONDON
ATLANTA MONTREUX SYDNEY

TWIST IN MY TALES: *Short Stories for Children*
Copyright © Marie Watts 1998

All Rights Reserved

No part of this book may be reproduced in any form
by photocopying or by any electronic or mechanical means,
including information storage or retrieval systems,
without permission in writing from both the copyright
owner and the publisher of this book.

ISBN 0 75410 485 0

First Published 1998 by
MINERVA PRESS
Sixth Floor
Canberra House
315–317 Regent Street
London W1R 7YB

Printed in Great Britain for Minerva Press

TWIST IN MY TALES
Short Stories for Children

Contents

Go, Frankie, Go!	7
Wheels for Legs	10
Selina's Crystal Ring	13
Sara's Late Call Out	16
Danger, Bully at Work	19
The Shadow	21
Starfire	24
Have Prisoner, With Care	27
Robbie's Second Chance	30
Baz Wins Through	32
The Talking Cloak	35
Journey to Nowhere	38

Go, Frankie, Go!

Frankie was a fox who had lived in the countryside ever since he was a cub. When he got very hungry and there wasn't enough to eat he would start to wander into the town to look for food, always returning to his home before dawn.

He didn't want people to spot him because he knew they would set their dogs on him, as they never understood that he wouldn't hurt them.

One night, Frankie was searching for food in town. Suddenly he heard a sniffing noise. Something was coming after him! He wondered if it could be a dog as he was very near a house. As the source of the noise got closer and closer he saw an outline of an animal. He knew it to be friendly; it was a badger who was just looking for food. He ignored it and carried on with his own searching.

A few minutes later he smelt something very tasty to eat. It was a mouse which had crawled under an upturned dustbin and had become trapped there. Frankie eased his nose underneath the dustbin. He lifted it just enough to get his mouth round the mouse to eat it. He crunched up its bones with his teeth and smacked his lips after he had swallowed it. Mice were one of his favourite types of food to eat.

Frankie thought he had better start back home to the countryside after his meal. It was already starting to get light and he couldn't risk hanging about. He began running fast and as he looked back he saw something he dreaded. It was a pair of feet with big black boots on them and they made a heavy thumping sound as they got closer and closer. Suddenly he saw a high wall and jumped over it. He was making for a hiding place known only to him. The boots went walking by, not knowing which way Frankie had gone.

A few days later Frankie woke up and thought to himself what a lovely day it was going to be. He didn't know how wrong his thoughts would turn out to be that afternoon.

As Frankie was crawling out of his home he pricked up his ears. He could hear some horse's hooves and hounds barking. He also heard a huntsman blowing a hunting horn in the distance. He put his nose up in the air to see if he could tell how far away they were and how much time he had to make his escape. He knew he couldn't stay where he was as he didn't want to give away the whereabouts of his home.

Frankie started to run. He tried to give the hounds a false scent trail but he didn't have much luck. The dogs were getting closer to him and they wouldn't give up.

Frankie then made for the part of the woods where the river ran through. When he arrived there he thought he had lost his pursuers. Very gently he walked into the water, not wanting to make any noise to alert the hounds. He swam across the river, but when he got to the other side he found a hound had broken away from the pack. She was waiting for him with her mouth wide open and her tongue hanging out, dripping with saliva. She pounced and had him in her jaws; she dug her teeth into his flesh and drew blood. He tried to pull free and as he did so he left some of his fur in her mouth.

After he got free he began running again – he hadn't any choice if he didn't want them to eat him alive. He started making for his secret hideaway, taking care he wasn't followed by the other hounds. He was getting weaker. He hadn't gone far when he collapsed due to loss of blood.

All of a sudden Frankie heard a familiar noise; that of the big black boots that had followed him in the town. The boots came to an abrupt halt.

Frankie felt something warm and soft being wrapped around his sore, bleeding body. He found himself being lifted and carried by the man who belonged to the boots. The man took Frankie back to his cottage to see if he could make him better. It was touch and go for Frankie, as the man had to use a needle and thread to sew his wound up. Then Frankie was put outside in a cage, as the man knew it would be cruel to keep the fox indoors.

It was a month before Frankie recovered enough even to walk again. The man had to coax him to have something to eat. After Frankie had started eating he began to get stronger. The man had to think about setting him free. It was a bright, sunny day when he let Frankie go and it took all of his courage to do so because he had grown very fond of the little fox. After he had carried the cage far enough away from his cottage he opened the cage door. Frankie stepped out, very slowly at first, sniffing the air. He wanted to make sure there weren't any hounds around before he ventured right out of the cage.

Frankie never knew that the man was an old fox-hunter who didn't have the nerve to kill him. When he was certain the way was clear of hounds, Frankie started to run. As he looked back he saw the man say, 'Go, Frankie, go!'

Wheels for Legs

While Stuart's parents were getting ready to go on a day trip, he went downstairs in the lift to wait in the hotel lounge. He sat next to a sweet old lady. He asked her if she was going on the trip. She replied that she wasn't because Pete the coach driver drove like a madman.

Stuart told his parents what the old lady had said about Pete. They didn't listen; they just made their way to the coach.

Pete started the engine and put his foot down on the accelerator. The coach sped along the narrow, rough mountain road. Everybody yelled at Pete to slow down. He didn't take any notice.

Stuart undid his seatbelt, got up and walked towards Pete. He asked him if he hadn't got more sense than to drive so fast on roads like these, but still Pete didn't listen.

Stuart was getting very scared. He tried to put his foot on the brake but Pete was too strong for him. He shoved Stuart off. As he did so, Pete's hand slipped from the steering wheel. The coach went out of control. It started to swerve. Pete tried to straighten it up. The coach got too close to the edge of the mountain road. It went crashing down the side of the mountain, rolling over and over.

It came to rest the right way up. As luck would have it, a car passed by shortly after the crash had happened. The driver climbed down to see if he could help. He tried opening the driver's door. It was stuck. He pulled and tugged at it until it came free. Then he climbed inside.

The man saw Stuart and asked if he could move at all. Stuart replied that he couldn't. He said his legs were trapped. The car driver had to climb back up the mountainside to call for the emergency services. He scrambled to the top. He knew it wouldn't be easy to find help on that lonely road so he got back into his car and drove about eight miles, until a cottage came into view. The driver asked the occupants if he could use their phone to call the emergency services. They wanted to know why and when he told them they offered to go back with him to where the accident had happened. When they got there, they climbed down the mountainside to get the other injured people out of the coach.

A rescue helicopter arrived and lowered a man on a winch. The rescuer had with him a stretcher, a neck brace and some cutting equipment. He hung above the coach, near to where Stuart's legs were trapped. He shouted to make sure that Stuart wasn't too close before he started cutting a hole in the roof of the coach big enough for him and Stuart to get through.

The rescuer lowered himself down and put the brace on Stuart's neck. He cut the crumpled dashboard where Stuart was trapped. He knew he had to be careful; he didn't know what other injuries Stuart had incurred.

After the rescuer had freed Stuart and fastened him on to the stretcher, he waved his hand to the helicopter pilot to winch them up. Then they flew to the hospital.

Stuart didn't know just how bad his legs were. The rescuer didn't have the heart to tell him. The surgeon met them and rushed Stuart straight into theatre for an operation on his legs.

When Stuart came round, the surgeon explained that his legs had been too badly damaged to save. Stuart was very upset as he had been in the school running team. The surgeon sent for Stuart's parents who were in the same hospital recovering from cuts and bruises. They consoled Stuart by telling him about very high powered electric wheelchairs and other aids. That seemed to do him good.

The next day Stuart asked if he could try an electric chair when he felt less sore. The surgeon told him he could. As he turned away he thought about how it would take Stuart a long time to adapt to his new life.

Selina's Crystal Ring

As the waves were crashing over the rocks Selina stood gazing out to sea. She was feeling very lonely because she had just moved into town from the country. She wondered if she would ever make any new friends.

She turned and began to walk slowly along the beach, kicking up the sand with her bare feet. Suddenly she noticed something shining in the sand. She bent down and picked it up. It was a pretty ring. She slipped it on one of her fingers.

As the sun shone it caught the crystal glass in the ring. The crystals dazzled Selina; her eyes glazed over and she felt giddy and passed out.

When she came round a few minutes later Selina sat up very slowly and rubbed and blinked her eyes. She had no idea where she was. She didn't know that the ring was magical and had the power to transport people backwards and forwards in time.

Selina glanced down to check if the ring was still on her finger. She saw that it was. She stood up and looked around her; she knew immediately that she wasn't in the same place as before. She was in a street full of people dressed in old-fashioned clothes.

Then Selina saw a small boy wearing very scruffy, dirty clothes, sitting huddled in a doorway. He looked like he wanted a square meal inside him. Selina went over and asked him what his name was. He said it was Sam and that he was an orphan. Selina then told him her name and what had happened with the ring. Sam told her that he thought she was mad. Selina showed him the crystal ring, being very careful not to let it shine into his eyes. She didn't want the same thing happening to him.

What Sam did next really shocked Selina. He snatched the ring right off her finger and ran away as fast as he could. Selina tried to catch up with him. She was getting very out of breath when she saw him disappear round a corner. She thought she would be trapped in that time for ever if she didn't get the ring back.

As Sam was running the ring slipped out of his hand on to the road. He stopped and looked for it, found it and then did something he shouldn't – he glanced at the shining crystals. He got the same glazed look in his eyes that Selina had before she was transported back in time.

Selina was still following Sam and stepped up to him as he was looking at the ring. As she did so she too got caught in the sparkling crystals of the ring. Both Sam and Selina began to feel dizzy and passed out. This time the ring worked in reverse.

When Sam and Selina came round they realised that it wasn't the same time as when they had looked at the ring. It had transported them back to the beach where Selina first found it, which meant big trouble for Sam. How was he going to explain his old-fashioned, scruffy clothes to people from this unfamiliar time?

Selina was trying to think of an explanation for Sam's way of dressing. All of a sudden she had a brainwave: she would tell people that Sam had been to a fancy dress party the night before and he'd not yet had the chance to change his clothes. When she told Sam about her plan, he said he thought it was a good idea.

They started walking slowly along the beach towards Selina's house. They spotted her neighbour called Vic. He could be a real pain. He was very nosy and constantly asking Selina to go out with him.

As Vic got closer he saw Sam. He eyed him up and down and asked Selina who the stranger was. She told him that Sam was her cousin from the next town. She then went on to explain why he was dressed as he was.

Then Vic saw the crystal ring Selina was wearing. Selina started to smile to herself. She was having a very wicked thought about how to get rid of Vic. She called him over as she knew it was his sister's birthday the following week and he would want something very special for her.

Selina took the ring off her finger to let Vic have a closer look at it. As he did so, the crystals started to sparkle.

Selina didn't see that Sam had crept up behind Vic. Both of them then started being transported back in time but before they completely disappeared, the ring slipped out of Vic's grasp. Selina picked it up from the ground, still being very careful not to look at the crystals, and put it back in her jacket pocket. She wondered if Sam had got back to his own time and whether Vic was now regretting being nosy. He might not return if Selina didn't look at her crystal ring ever again. Who knew?

Sara's Late Call Out

It was a lovely sunny day when Sara started her first job as a vet's assistant. She was really looking forward to working with animals and she loved the countryside where Phil the vet had his own surgery. Sara knew she would get on well with him; he was very kind and had been patient with her when she had gone for the job interview.

The first thing Phil asked Sara to do was get a dog ready for an operation. After she had done this he told her she could assist with the operation, if she felt confident enough. She said that she would very much like to do so as they were only going to take out two decayed teeth which were very painful for the poor dog.

In the afternoon Phil offered to take Sara out with him on his rounds. She jumped at the chance to learn more about the job.

Their first call was at a farm to see a cow which had an infection on her side where she had caught it on some barbed wire. Phil asked Sara what she thought they should do. She replied that she would open the wound to let the poison out and then put some antiseptic on it. If the wound was large she would stitch it up. Phil told her that was correct and patted her on the back.

Their next call was on an old lady who had a cat which was having difficulty breathing. While Phil was examining the cat its heart suddenly stopped beating. Phil began rubbing the cat's chest very gently and, slowly, it started to come round. Sara looked across at Phil. He just shook his head. He didn't want to upset the old lady as there wasn't much hope left for her cat.

Sara took the old lady into another room to explain that her cat might not last the night. Sara put her arm around the old lady and told her to phone Phil if the cat got worse again. The old lady said she would do what Sara had suggested before Sara told her that she had to go to help Phil with his other calls.

In the middle of the night Phil rang Sara to ask her to help him with an accident involving a young dog which had been hit by a car. While they were driving there Phil told Sara that the old lady's cat had died.

They got to the scene of the accident and Sara could see that the dog was in a bad way. While she stroked the dog to calm it down, Phil managed to stop the bleeding. Then he asked Sara to help him lift the dog into his car as he had to take it back to the surgery. The dog's ribs were broken and it also had trouble with its vision.

When they got back to the surgery, Phil told Sara to hold the dog tight while he bandaged its ribs. Then he looked into the dog's eyes. They were clearing quickly. The dog had a very sad expression on its face as if to say, 'Please don't hurt me.' Then it started to lick Phil's hand.

A few weeks later, when the injured dog was feeling better, Sara took it for a walk and saw the old lady who had lost her cat. Sara told her about the dog's accident and that it hadn't got an owner. The old lady asked her if she could have the dog for company as she had been very lonely since her cat had gone. Sara said she would ask Phil.

When Sara got back to the surgery, she told Phil what the old lady had asked her. He said that she could have the dog with pleasure as he didn't like to think of her being on her own.

Sara took the dog to the old lady. When she saw her new pet, tears of joy filled her eyes. The dog jumped up and licked them off her face. Sara knew the two of them would never be lonely again.

Danger, Bully at Work

Carl's mum shouted upstairs to her son that he would be late for school if he didn't hurry up. He yelled back that he was just coming.

Carl dreaded going to school. His lessons were boring and never seemed to change. However, that wasn't the only thing he hated about his school. When Carl first started, he had really loved the school, but then came Zak who did nothing but cause trouble. He kept picking on the smaller kids by demanding their dinner money. When they didn't pay up Zak clouted them. The children were very scared of Zak.

Carl was trying to think of a way to stop Zak. It wasn't going to be easy to trap him; Zak was too clever to get caught at his bullying. He always did it out of sight of the teachers.

Later that day Carl saw Zak had pinned Nicky up against a wall and was hitting him. Tears were streaming down Nicky's cheeks. Carl rushed over to him to try to get Zak off Nicky, but he was too strong for Carl. Then Zak swung round and began punching Carl in the stomach. Carl clutched himself in pain before starting to fight back, letting fly with both fists. He knocked Zak to the ground and managed to get Nicky away to safety.

Carl went back to his home to get himself and Nicky cleaned up before their parents saw the mess they were in. Nicky washed his face and it really didn't look too bad apart from a small cut above his left eye. Luckily his hair would hide it.

Carl had a big bruise on his stomach where Zak had been thumping him. Carl knew he had to do something to stop Zak before it was too late.

The following day Carl saw Zak picking on somebody else. Zak was just going to snatch the kid's dinner money when he spotted Carl walking towards him with a strange look in his eyes. Carl looked furious.

Zak started to run away very quickly. Carl went after him and caught him up around the corner. He grabbed Zak by the jacket and told him that if he didn't stop his bullying he would be reported. Zak just laughed in Carl's face, and pulled his jacket free. He walked away, laughing in a very big-headed manner.

A few hours later, Carl heard a loud cry. It was Nicky, who was being chased by Zak. Carl saw that a teacher was looking out of a window. Now he had to make sure that the teacher saw what happened next. Carl caught the teacher's eye, who nodded back.

Zak had got Nicky by the scruff of the neck and was shaking him hard. He was going through Nicky's pockets, looking for money. When he couldn't find any he banged Nicky's head against the wall.

By this time the teacher had seen what Zak had done. He rushed out to rescue Nicky. He examined Nicky's head. It had a large bump on it, but apart from that he looked all right.

The teacher told Zak that he was going to recommend to the board of governors that he should be expelled for his bullying. He marched Zak out of the school gates and said he didn't want to see him there again, unless Zak was with his parents.

Carl and Nicky were very pleased to hear that Zak wouldn't bother them any more. Things would be better now they had got rid of the school bully.

The Shadow

An owl hooted and the wind whistled through the trees. Terror welled up inside Kerry as she thought she saw a shadow of somebody creeping about in the graveyard where she was taking a short cut home from the Girl Guides. It was very dark and creepy in that place at night.

Kerry started to run and whatever she had sensed followed her. She turned round to try to spot what or who it was but she was too slow as it dived behind a gravestone. She had heard rumours of a prowler, hanging around, and she thought it might be him.

The church clock was striking ten o'clock. Kerry knew her parents would be very worried by now as the Guides finished at nine. She always arrived home fifteen minutes afterwards. Where had the shadow gone? she wondered, as it wasn't anywhere to be seen.

When Kerry got to the end of the graveyard she felt a hand on her shoulder. She shivered and turned round to see the outline of a man with long hair, shrouded in a thin mist.

Kerry thought he was a prowler. She started screaming. The man disappeared into thin air and Kerry couldn't believe her eyes. She continued to run home – not knowing that he was still following her.

When she got home, her parents asked why she was late. She told them. They looked at each other in a very strange way. It was as if they knew something she didn't.

The next day Kerry went to school and she told her

friend Gina what had happened. Gina asked Kerry if she would be walking home through the graveyard again. Kerry said of course she would as it was the quickest way from her house. Gina said she would go with her next time.

A week later Gina called for Kerry to walk with her to Guides. Gina wanted to see if what had followed Kerry would do so again tonight.

The two girls reached the graveyard. Suddenly the shadow appeared. He was standing, watching Gina's every movement. An ice-cold shiver ran down her back. She just stood and stared at the man. Then she shouted to Kerry to come quick. Kerry ran up the graveyard path, looking pale.

When Kerry saw the shadow she plucked up the courage to ask him who he was. He said if she didn't know him she must ask her parents; then he faded away again.

Gina took Kerry home. She wasn't in any fit state to go to Guides.

When Kerry got home she started to ask her parents about the shadow. They said that they would tell her all about it in the morning.

When Kerry woke up the next day, she just couldn't wait to hear what her parents had to say. She went downstairs for breakfast and her mum asked her if she was all right. Kerry said she would be if they told her why the shadow kept appearing to her.

Kerry's parents sat her down and began to explain that her real dad was buried in that graveyard. He had been killed while he was on his way to the hospital to watch her being born. It sounded like it was his ghost wanting to see what Kerry looked like.

Kerry started to cry. She had never guessed her present dad had adopted her when he married her mum. She told her parents she was going back to the graveyard to confront the shadow.

The next night Kerry walked to where she had seen the

shadow and, sure enough, he appeared. She told him that her real parents had explained how her real dad died. She asked the shadow if he was her dad. He answered that he was. She asked him why he had come back to haunt her. He said it was just to find out what she looked like and if she was all right. She said that she was very happy with her mum and adopted dad. The shadow said that he was now content and wouldn't bother her any more. He then started to fade away. Kerry yelled after him that she would always love him. She hoped he had heard her. The shadow gave her a wave and was gone, but she had a feeling it wasn't going to be for ever.

Starfire

When Starfire was a foal she had used to run around a big, grassy field. She had enjoyed being in the open air but all that had changed now Starfire was fully grown. Now she was working as a pit pony in the local coal mine. She really missed feeling the sun on her back. Alex, the lad who worked with and looked after Starfire, knew this, and brought her little treats like apples and mints. Starfire wished she could run away, but she knew she would never do so. Alex might get into trouble if she did.

Starfire pulled heavy mining trucks filled with large lumps of coal to which Alex had to hitch her up every morning. One day, while he was doing this he heard a rumbling noise. He thought it was just a thunderstorm and decided to ignore it.

Starfire tossed her head and neighed very wildly. She sensed it was something more than thunder. The rumbling stopped. Alex thought the storm must have ended.

Suddenly the mine shook. A pit prop was starting to collapse and thick, black coal dust was coming down from the ceiling, making it very hard for the miners and ponies to see and breathe. Two more pit props were also starting to fall, threatening to bring down the whole of the pit roof.

It was panic stations down there. The miners were scrambling to get out. They didn't know the exit was blocked with huge lumps of coal, rocks and pieces of wooden pit prop.

Starfire pounded the debris with her hooves. It didn't do

much good. She went to where Alex lay. He couldn't move at all because a pit prop was lying across his chest, making it hard for him to breathe.

A miner came to try to help Starfire move the prop. It was too heavy for him to lift; a large rock had broken one of his arms.

Then the miner tried to clear the debris from the exit. The huge rocks were too awkward for him to move but he managed to clear some of the smaller ones.

Starfire came to see if the miner would like to throw them into her truck, to which she was still hooked. As the miner started to put some of the rocks that he could manage to lift into the truck, he suddenly saw a glimmer of sunlight, which made him work even faster. He heard the sound of voices. They seemed to be coming from down the tunnel. It was some of the other miners, who had been trapped in the second half of the mine but had managed to get free. The first miner let them know he was all right; then he pointed to where Alex was pinned down. The others rushed over and very carefully pulled the pit prop off Alex's chest. It had broken one of his ribs.

Very gently they put Alex into Starfire's truck, ready for when the exit had been cleared. They wouldn't want to hang about as there wasn't much air left. It had been two hours since the exit had become blocked.

Suddenly they heard the sound of a drill coming from above. They saw a bit of sky. Some of the men outside started helping to remove the debris. They wanted to get the trapped men out quickly.

A huge cheer went up when the men in the mine saw their rescuers. One of the miners lead Starfire towards the exit. She was getting very excited as she started to smell the fresh air again.

The people who owned the coal mine decided that because Starfire had stood by her men she would be allowed to retire to an open field to spend the rest of her life.

Have Prisoner, With Care

Wendy was getting near to the café where she went every day for her lunch before returning to the office. Suddenly a police car went speeding by with its siren blaring out. Wendy looked and wondered if they had recaptured Rick, the escaped prisoner who had been on the run from the detention centre for two days.

She couldn't understand why Rick had turned to crime when his parents were rich and he could have had anything he wanted. Rick had always been a caring lad when he was at school but after he had left he had joined a gang of lads who were unemployed and only interested in having some money in their pockets.

Rick had got caught with a video recorder in his arms whilst leaving a house the gang had been robbing. The other lads had run away before the police arrived.

Wendy went into the café and ordered something to eat. Just after she had sat down, the café door burst open and there stood Rick. He snatched up a knife from a table and waved it about madly. He told Wendy to stop screaming. He looked around for food, spotted a sandwich, and pushed it into his mouth.

Rick went over to Wendy. He put one hand over her mouth, and with the other held the knife to her throat. He dragged her out of the door. He took her round the corner to a van that he had stolen, opened the door and pushed her inside; then he drove off to the country.

Wendy guessed they were heading for Mark's. Mark had

been Rick's best friend at school. Rick could always rely on Mark when he was in trouble.

When they reached Mark's house Rick got out of the van, went round to Wendy's side and pulled her out of the door. They went to the back door and Rick banged on it. When Mark saw them he said they couldn't stay as the police were on their way over. Rick said that all he wanted was some food. Suddenly they heard the police car siren coming along the road.

Rick panicked. He grabbed Wendy, ran to the van and shoved her in. He got in and drove away.

The police saw the van and began to follow it. Rick put his foot down hard on the accelerator, trying to outrun his pursuers. As he was overtaking the car in front of him, he almost failed to see the lorry coming the other way. At the last moment he swerved to avoid it. They ran head-on into a tree.

Wendy went crashing through the windscreen and landed on the hard ground. Rick was knocked out for a few minutes. When he came round he saw that Wendy was very badly hurt. He went to see if he could help her.

Wendy didn't respond when Rick spoke to her. He gave her the kiss of life – that brought her round. He knew it was too dangerous to move her. He then took a hanky out of his pocket and dabbed her face with it. He made sure she was comfortable before he went looking for a phone. It wasn't easy for him to walk as he had a large cut on his leg. Luckily he found a house not far from the crash. He rang for an ambulance.

Rick didn't know that while he was doing this, the police had turned up. When he returned he decided to give himself up. Wendy told the policemen what had happened, and how Rick had taken care of her after the accident. She hoped it would help in his defence in court.

A few weeks later Rick's case came to court. Wendy

went in and saw Rick in the dock; he looked terrible. She was there to give evidence in his defence.

When the judge came in he told Rick that stealing was bad enough, but kidnapping was much more serious. Looking straight at Rick the judge said that Wendy had spoken up in his defence, and this had been taken into consideration when Rick's sentence had been decided. That was why the judge had given Rick just two years' community service at an old people's home.

Rick started working there and enjoyed it very much. Wendy was pleased about that; she thought that perhaps he would go back to being the caring lad he used to be before he turned to crime.

Robbie's Second Chance

The road was deserted as Amy strolled along it. She had expected it to be busy but she didn't pass any kids. Amy thought that perhaps they had gone to welcome back Robbie from hospital. He had a rough time with his blood cancer and his only hope was a successful bone marrow transplant.

Robbie had been waiting weeks for a bone marrow donor. Even if one was found, he had been told there was no guarantee the operation would work.

The hospital had sent for Robbie because a donor had become available on their register. Robbie had gone into the hospital very hopeful that the transplant was going to be a success.

The donor didn't want Robbie to know who had given the bone marrow. He or she had arranged with the hospital that his or her name remained a secret.

When the day came for Robbie to have his transplant operation, he was very excited. The doctor tried to calm him down, which was impossible under the circumstances. Robbie had been ill since he was born.

It wasn't very long before they were ready for him in theatre.

After the operation Robbie was very sleepy. He didn't see the secret donor peep in the ward window to see how he was getting on.

The donor was pleased that he looked so much better, although aware that it was early days, and many things could still go wrong.

A few weeks later, when he had got a lot stronger, the hospital let Robbie go home.

Amy had thought she would go to visit Robbie and had walked to where he lived. As she got near she could hear squeals of laughter coming from the house. His parents were having a party for Robbie. He was enjoying himself when suddenly he felt dizzy and passed out. Immediately his mum phoned for an ambulance.

The ambulance came soon after. Robbie was rushed to the hospital. He was very sick because his body was rejecting the transplant. The doctor started giving him some special drugs to help stop the rejection. It looked like they were starting to work and he began to come round. He asked for his mum. When she came in, she told him that the doctors had stopped the rejection just in time and he was a very lucky lad to have such clever doctors like that.

When Robbie felt like having other visitors, Amy went to see him. She asked him if he was feeling better. He said he felt great and couldn't wait to go home again.

Robbie's parents had planned a day trip to the zoo to celebrate his homecoming. They invited Amy to come along too. Amy said she would love to go with them as she had something important to tell Robbie.

When they got to the zoo Robbie wanted to see everything. He took Amy to see his favourite chimps, which were swinging on their tyres. After that they went to the zebra enclosure. There Amy asked Robbie if she could have a word with him in private. He was puzzled and asked her why. Amy told him that she was his secret donor; she had been a perfect match on the hospital register. Amy explained that she couldn't tell him before as she didn't know whether the transplant would be a success.

After she had told him, Robbie thanked her for giving him a second chance of life.

Baz Wins Through

It was a very nasty, wet night when Baz the badger woke up. He poked his little black nose out of his underground home, sniffing the damp air. He nearly changed his mind about going out to search for food. He was starving; he had no choice but to brave the rainy night. That wasn't the only thing that he had to worry about. Rosy the dog was also out to get him for his master Mr King, who lived in a farm near the dark, creepy wood where Baz had his underground home.

Mr King was a very rough man and was also very cruel to Rosy. He used to beat her when she failed to catch Baz. It wasn't Rosy's fault that Baz could run faster and find lots of hiding places to get away from her.

Baz's stomach was getting more and more empty, so he very carefully stepped out to find something to eat. He knew his special friend Sally would never let him down. She always left some scraps of food for him on the path near his home.

Baz made his way towards the pathway, using his nose as a guide because his eyesight was poor. Suddenly, he heard heavy footsteps coming up behind him. It was Mr King!

Baz couldn't hear any barking or panting. Where was Rosy? She might be waiting to pounce on him. That really scared Baz because if Rosy ever caught him she would tear him to pieces.

By now it was very misty. That was ideal for Baz; it

would make it easier for him to evade capture if Rosy got his scent.

Baz lost track of Mr King's footsteps, forgetting that Rosy's master was searching for him.

All of a sudden, Baz could sense a pair of eyes staring straight at him. He tensed and then realised it was just Sally putting some food down for him. In his eagerness he didn't see that someone was standing behind her with a spade in his hand.

It was Mr King, waiting to hit Baz on his head. Sally became aware that something was wrong. Quickly she turned, just in time to stop the spade from hitting Baz. She snatched it from Mr King's hands and smacked him in the face with it. He fell to the ground very hard, hitting his head on a huge rock as he did so. He lay with blood pouring from his wound. He wasn't moving at all. Sally realised she had to get help fast so she ran to the farm to ring for an ambulance.

When she arrived, Rosy stood by the door growling and baring her teeth. Sally thought quickly and looked down for stones to throw at the dog to scare her off. It was too dark for her to see.

Sally heard a noise coming from the farm drive: she thought it was Baz. Mr King was still flat out. She thought about fifteen minutes had passed since she had left him but she couldn't be sure.

Sally was scared as the noise got closer and closer, although it sounded less and less like a man's footsteps. She heaved a sigh of relief when she spotted Baz's bright eyes through the dark.

Baz made sure Rosy could see him. She moved menacingly towards him but he was too fast for her, and took a running jump at her, sinking his sharp teeth deep into the dog's neck. Yelping with pain, Rosy ran off into the wood.

While Baz dealt with Rosy, Sally managed to get inside

and ring for the ambulance. She wanted to make sure Mr King hadn't moved so she made her way back to the wood. It was a very dense wood and she didn't want the ambulancemen to get lost.

Sally heard the siren coming along the road beside the wood. She waited by the side of the road to show them where Mr King was lying.

Suddenly Sally caught sight of the ambulance's headlights coming round the bend. Sally started waving madly to catch the attention of the driver. The ambulance stopped where she stood and one of the ambulancemen asked how Mr King was. She told them he was bleeding a lot and showed the way.

Sally hoped that they would make it in time. There was no need to worry as Mr King was sitting up against a tree, wiping his face. The ambulancemen treated his deep cuts and looked at his head. They insisted he went to the hospital with them for a more detailed examination.

Mr King and Sally got in the ambulance. Sally explained what had happened to Rosy. She also told Mr King how Baz had saved his life by getting rid of Rosy. Mr King promised never to hunt Baz again. Even though Mr King was her dad, Sally never told him that she fed Baz.

The Talking Cloak

Cobwebs were hanging from the ceiling and wafting in the breeze from the broken windows in the house that had been for sale for years. Nobody wanted to buy it as everyone in the area thought it was haunted.

A young couple named Dale and Lyn went to view the house. They thought it was just what they wanted, even though it needed a lot of repairs. That was before they knew what they had let themselves in for, after they had moved in.

The trouble began a few nights after they had settled in. They were sitting in the lounge watching the TV when suddenly Dale heard creaking noises coming from upstairs. He went to investigate every room. He didn't find anything; he just felt an icy chill in the bedroom where they slept. He told Lyn that there was nothing to be scared of. He never said anything about what he had felt as he didn't want to frighten her.

The next night their problems really began. When Lyn got up for a glass of water she saw a cloak floating towards her. She dropped the glass she was holding and it smashed on the floor. She screamed at the top of her voice. Dale came running out of their bedroom, wondering what he would find. Lyn pointed a trembling finger at what she thought was the cloak.

All Dale saw was a white cat walking along the landing. He picked up the cat and put it outside. Then he felt the same icy chill as before. Lyn felt it too and shivered. She gave Dale a puzzled look; she wasn't sure if it had been just her imagination.

Lyn told Dale what she had seen. She asked him what he thought had happened. He said it might have been just a stray cat that had come in through an open window, and that with all the dark corners the house had it wasn't very surprising that Lyn should think she saw a cloak floating about late at night. He said they should go back to bed and try to get some sleep.

That night it was hard for Lyn to fall asleep again. She kept thinking she could hear strange noises coming from the next room.

All of a sudden the cloak appeared again. This time it came into their bedroom. It floated round to where Lyn lay. She went stiff with fright as the cloak started to speak to her. It said it needed Lyn's help to get back to its owner, who had worked as a nurse in the First World War. She had died of her wounds about ninety years ago after a bomb had exploded in her face while she was tending the injured.

When Lyn had recovered sufficiently, she said that she would see what she could find out about the cloak's owner. The cloak then floated away and the white cat that Lyn had seen a few hours ago returned before wandering off.

The following day Lyn went to the library to find out how old the house was. She discovered it was over one hundred and fifty years old. That meant the cloak's owner must have lived there before the war. Lyn asked the librarian if the house's owner had been a nurse in the First World War. The librarian went to have a look in their records, and sure enough everything the cloak had said was true. What the cloak never knew was that after the nurse had died she had turned into a white cat – the same cat that kept coming back to the house.

Lyn went home to wait for nightfall. She wanted to tell the cloak what she had found out about its owner's secret;

then perhaps it would stop haunting their house. Or would it?

Journey to Nowhere

Sean's journey had really started seven months ago when the stranger called Mr Harris came to stay in the hotel where Sean lived with his parents. Mr Harris had just purchased a racing stable and needed somewhere to stay while he sorted out his business.

Mr Harris was looking for a lad he could train to be an apprentice steeplechasing jockey. He wasn't having much luck until he saw Sean, whom he thought was the right height and weight for a jockey. Mr Harris asked Sean if he would be interested in riding horses. Sean said he had never tried. Mr Harris then told Sean he could come to the stables to see how he sat on a horse and said that if he was any good he might like to start training with him to be a proper racing jockey.

Mr Harris took Sean to the stables the next morning and showed him around. Sean was very impressed with the place. He asked Mr Harris if he could sit on a horse and Mr Harris shouted to a stable lad named Mike to get the horse called Holly out for Sean as she was very gentle and perfect for someone who had never ridden a horse before.

Mike led Holly to where Sean stood. Holly then put her nose in Sean's hand. He stroked her ears. Mike helped Sean on to Holly's back and Sean nearly slipped off. Mike managed to catch him in time. He told Sean to hold on tight to the reins. He walked them around the paddock very slowly. Then he asked Sean if he would care to have a go on his own. Sean replied he would like to very much as he was enjoying riding by himself. He felt in complete control of Holly. He dug his heels into her belly to make her go faster. She began to gallop hard around the paddock until she got to the fence around it; then she raised her front legs and jumped the fence, taking Sean with her. He was hanging on to the reins so tightly that his hands were starting to bleed and his whole body ached with the strain of trying to stay on Holly's back.

They landed on the other side of the fence. Mike caught up with them and told Sean off for doing such a stupid thing for his first time on a horse. Even though he was wearing a safety helmet, Mike said, he could still have been killed.

Mike explained to Mr Harris what Sean had done. Mr Harris was annoyed at first; then he thought for a moment. He badly wanted a steeplechase jockey. He asked to see Sean. When Sean came Mr Harris then told him he was very angry with him for risking Holly's life and his own as she wasn't even a jumper. He said he was going to give Sean another chance provided he didn't do any more silly tricks. Sean then promised he wouldn't do it again.

After Sean had done his training Mr Harris gave him his first proper ride. It was on a horse called Armour. Mr Harris thought Sean would be the best person to handle that horse as Armour was very difficult to control and needed somebody who was tough enough not to let him get his own way.

The time had come for their first race and while they were waiting for the nine other horses to come up to the starting line, Sean spotted Mike behaving in a very strange manner. When Mike saw Sean watching him he looked guilty and he ran off.

After the race, in which he came in second, Sean went looking for Mike. He found him in the horsebox of Mr Harris's best steeplechaser.

Mike was staring into space when Sean spoke to him. He swung round and started thumping Sean, who began hitting him back. Sean grabbed Mike's wrist, making him drop the thing he was holding. Sean saw that it was a full syringe. He knew that it would mean trouble if he didn't stop Mike.

He hit Mike hard, knocking him out for a few seconds.

Sean picked up the syringe and put it in his pocket. When Mike came round Sean asked him why he tried to dope one of the greatest ever jumpers. Mike said he needed extra cash fast as his house would be repossessed if he didn't get some more money soon.

While they were fighting they hadn't noticed Mr Harris come in. He didn't hear what Mike told Sean; he just saw Sean put the syringe in his pocket. He thought to himself: Is that the way Sean repays people for giving him a chance of a job?

After a few hours Mr Harris sent for Sean, who tried to explain that it was Mike who was trying to dope the horse and not him. Mr Harris didn't believe him as Mike had been working at the stables for years. Mr Harris said he had two choices: the first being to call the police, the second to sack Sean and make sure he never got another ride in this country.

As Sean climbed the steps of the plane he wondered why he had to leave the place he had loved since he was a kid, just for trying to help a friend. He knew he wouldn't have another chance to be a jockey, so it was just a journey to nowhere.